Achieving QTS

Primary English: Audit and Test

Assessing your knowledge and understanding

Third Edition

Doreen Challen

Learning Matters

First published in 2001 by Learning Matters Ltd.
Reprinted in 2002.
Second edition published in 2003.
Reprinted in 2003.
Reprinted in 2004.
Reprinted in 2005.
Reprinted in 2006.
Third edition published in 2007.

British Library Cataloguing in Publication Data
A CIP record for this book is available from the British Library.

ISBN 978 1 84445 110 4

Cover design by Topics – The Creative Partnership
Text design by Code 5 Design Associates Ltd
Project Management by Deer Park Productions, Tavistock
Typeset by PDQ Typesetting Ltd, Newcastle-under-Lyme
Printed and bound in Great Britain by The Cromwell Press Ltd, Trowbridge, Wiltshire.

Learning Matters Ltd
33 Southernhay East
Exeter EX1 1NX
Tel: 01392 215560
Email: info@learningmatters.co.uk
www.learningmatters.co.uk

Contents

Introduction

About this book

This book has been written to support the subject knowledge learning of all primary trainee teachers on courses of Initial Teacher Training in England and other parts of the UK where a secure subject knowledge and understanding of English is required for the award of Qualified Teacher Status (QTS). In order to plan and teach effective English lessons, and to assess pupils' learning, it is vital that you have a secure subject knowledge and understanding of how the English language works, and feel confident in this. The audit and test materials presented here will help you to identify your own strengths and weaknesses in English. As you revise, you can revisit these to help you monitor and evaluate your own progress towards QTS:

Part 1 Your English background;
Part 2 Your interest in English;
Part 3 Audit: your perceived competence and confidence in English;
Part 4 English test;
Part 5 Answers to test questions;
Part 6 Targets for further development;
Part 7 Revision and further reading.

It is quite likely that your ITT provider will require you to further audit and test your subject knowledge and understanding of English as you start your course. You may wish to retain the results from this audit and test for your own records, using them for revision purposes. Your ITT provider may also wish to use them for their own records.

You may feel confident that, as a sophisticated user of English, possibly already having completed a degree, you already meet or exceed the subject knowledge expectations for a primary teacher. If so, you should find the test easy, and can go on with added confidence to develop your teaching skills. On the other hand, you may feel rather daunted, perhaps because it's been some time since you thought about how the English language works, or because you're aware that there are many aspects required nowadays which you didn't learn at school yourself. If so, there's no need to worry. After you've carried out this audit and test, you'll be able to pinpoint those areas which you will need to study further if you are to feel confident in the classroom, and then you can start to address your particular needs.

If you wish to revise, or feel the need for an English study aid, there are several excellent books written specifically for this purpose for primary trainees. *Primary English: Knowledge and Understanding* (third edition) from the *Learning Matters Achieving QTS Series* is particularly recommended. (See also the suggested reading in Part 7.)

The Standards for Qualified Teacher Status (2007)

A statutory framework for the career-long professional development of teachers has been designed by the Training and Development Agency for Schools (TDA). Within this wider framework, national standards for Qualified Teacher Status (QTS) are specified which trainee teachers must meet if they are to be awarded QTS.

These include, as aspects of professional knowledge and understanding, the requirements for trainee teachers to know and understand the *National Curriculum for English* and the Primary National Strategy (PNS) *Framework for Literacy*, and to have a secure knowledge and understanding of the English curriculum as appropriate to the age range for which they are trained. The audit and test materials in this book include many aspects of the specific English subject knowledge which you will need to know and understand in order to plan, teach and assess within these frameworks.

In terms of the professional skills set out in the Standards, it is vital that your subject knowledge is sufficiently secure for you to feel confident in teaching and assessing children's learning. Strong subject knowledge will enable you to understand the concepts you teach so that you can explain them effectively and offer examples, and help your pupils to investigate them and develop their own understandings. Strong subject knowledge will enable you to identify specifically what your pupils can do, and what they need to learn next. It will help you devise effective questions and provide feedback to move learning on.

The Standards also require you to show that you are beginning to address your personal professional development through taking steps to identify and meet your own professional needs. This book, by helping you to identify particular areas of subject knowledge for further study, has been designed to help you do this.

The audit and test materials cover:

- **the nature and role of standard English;**
- **the spoken and written language systems of English at word, sentence and text levels;**
- **evaluating texts and language critically;**
- **technical terms necessary to discuss English.**

English: the statutory framework

The National Curriculum for England (1999)

Schools have a statutory duty to teach the National Curriculum, which was first introduced in 1989. It is organised on the basis of four Key Stages, of which Key Stage 1 for 5–7 year-olds (Years 1 and 2) and Key Stage 2 for 7–11 year-olds (Years 3-6) cover the primary years. The *National Curriculum* for each Key Stage includes Programmes of Study which set out the English that children should be taught, and Attainment Targets, a series of level descriptions which provide a basis for making judgements about pupils' performance. The English Programmes of Study currently comprise:

- **En1: Speaking and Listening;**
- **En2: Reading;**
- **En3: Writing.**

The Foundation Stage

The scope of the National Curriculum was extended in 2002 to incorporate the Foundation Stage, introduced two years earlier as a distinct stage of education for children aged from 3 to 5. The Early Years curriculum, set out in *Curriculum Guidance for the Foundation Stage* (2000), covers six broad areas of learning, including 'Communication, Language and Literacy'. Statutory early learning goals describe what children are expected to achieve in these areas by the end of the Reception year, and provide the basis for the Early Years curriculum. In Autumn 2008, the Foundation Stage becomes part of the new Early Years Foundation Stage, covering care, learning and development for children in all early years settings from birth to the age of five.

English: the non-statutory framework

The Primary National Strategy

The Primary National Strategy (PNS) was established in 2003. While the existing National Literacy Strategy (NLS), introduced in 1998 with the aim of raising standards in literacy, retained a central place, the PNS broadened the focus of attention to learning and teaching across the full primary curriculum. The web-based *Primary Framework for Literacy* (2006) sets out end-of-year learning objectives across twelve strands, superseding the previous NLS *Framework for Teaching* (1998). Although schools are not legally required to use this framework, it interprets and develops the statutory curriculum, and is intended to promote progression and coherence from Reception year through to the end of primary schooling. A vast amount of associated guidance is available.

Many terms used in this book can be related directly to *Framework* objectives and to associated guidance materials, while others relate to concepts which will underpin your teaching of English more generally.

References

DfES (2006) *Primary Framework for Literacy and Mathematics*. London: DfES. Available online at http://www.standards.dfes.gov.uk/primaryframeworks/literacy/

DfEE/QCA (1998) *National Literacy Strategy Framework for Teaching*. London: HMSO.

DfEE/QCA (1999) *English: the National Curriculum for England*. London: HMSO.

DfEE/QCA (2000) *Curriculum Guidance for the Foundation Stage*. London: QCA.

Medwell, J., Moore, G., Wray, D. and Griffiths, V. (2007) *Primary English: Knowledge and Understanding* (3rd ed.) Exeter: Learning Matters.

TDA (2007) *Standards for the recommendation of Qualified Teacher Status*. London: TDA. Available online at http://www.tda.gov.uk/

Part 1: English background

Provide as many background details as you can. Don't worry if it looks blank in places; however, don't undersell yourself – although of course your English qualifications are important, many wider aspects of your education and life may be relevant. For example, familiarity with other languages, or a job that involves a lot of reading and writing, is bound to enhance your knowledge of how the English language is used.

▶ **personal details**

Name
Date of birth
Year(s) of course
Subject specialism
Key Stages

▶ **English qualifications and experience**

GCSE/O level (equivalent)

Date taken

Grade(s)

GCE A level (equivalent)

Date taken

Grade(s)

English degree

Year of graduation

Class of degree

Other English courses

▶ **other relevant qualifications** (e.g. TEFL)

▶ **other relevant experience** (e.g. work-related)

Part 2 Interest in English

How you feel about English will influence how you choose to develop your subject knowledge, and also the effectiveness of your teaching. An enthusiastic teacher who communicates his or her own enjoyment of language and literature to pupils will go a long way towards inspiring them to be lovers of language. You may not at the present moment be an English enthusiast, even if you're an expert user of the language! However, it is important to take an objective look at your attitudes. You may also find it useful to try to work out the reasons for the way you feel – for example, why do you think you enjoy reading but hate writing? Does this stem from your experiences at school, or elsewhere? Have your interests changed over time? Tick the appropriate columns:

	1 Very interested, enthusiastic	**2** Interested	**3** Not very interested	**4** Uninterested, unenthusiastic
Reading fiction				
Reading non-fiction				
Reading poetry				
Writing				
Speaking and listening activities (e.g. drama, poetry, debates)				
How language works				
Playing with words (e.g. puns, crosswords, puzzles)				

Overall, what do your responses tell you? If you've marked mostly 1s and 2s, that's an excellent start. 3s are encouraging, and even if you have some 4s, don't worry – everyone's different, and perhaps you'll come to feel more positive towards English as you progress through your ITT course. Reflect critically on your attitude towards English, using the space below to comment further. Can you identify the experiences which gave rise to your interest, or lack of it?

experiences statement

Part 3 Perceived competence and confidence in English

Competence is not the same as confidence – you may find, as you work through the following sections, that you feel very *competent* in certain areas of English, but currently don't feel *confident* about teaching it. By the end of your training, you will feel much stronger in both aspects.

If you use pencil in the sections that follow, you will be able to revisit the audit and test at a later date to assess your progress.

Competence

Use the key below to summarise how you perceive your own competence in relation to different aspects of English.

Please note: if you don't fully understand what some of the terms mean at present, don't worry about it – that in itself shows you're not going to award yourself a 1! You are not at present *expected* to know about, or feel competent in, everything listed here.

1 = Very good. Perceive existing competence as *exceeding* the stated expectation.

2 = Good. Perceive existing competence as *meeting* the stated expectation *comfortably*.

3 = Adequate. Perceive existing competence as *meeting* the stated expectation but *some* uncertainties still exist.

4 = Not good. Perceive existing competence as *not meeting* the stated expectation.

The nature and role of standard English

1 2 3 4

To underpin and support the effective teaching of primary English you should know and understand the nature and role of standard English as the medium through which all subjects are taught and as the common form of English used to communicate within the United Kingdom and throughout the English-speaking world.

1   2   3   4

The spoken and written language systems of English

1 2 3 4

To underpin and support the effective teaching of primary English you should know and understand the spoken and written language systems of English:

At word level:

- **phonics and how the writing system represents the sound system**   1   2   3   4
- **morphology – word structure and derivations**   1   2   3   4
- **word meanings and how words relate to each other**   1   2   3   4

At sentence level:

- **the grammar of spoken and written English**, including:
  - ▸ the grammatical function of words and phrases in clauses and sentences   1   2   3   4
  - ▸ word order and cohesion within sentences   1   2   3   4
  - ▸ types of sentences – statements, questions, commands, exclamations   1   2   3   4
  - ▸ simple, compound and complex sentences in writing   1   2   3   4
- **punctuation** – its main functions and conventions   1   2   3   4

At text level:

- **cohesion** – the way that individual words, sentences and paragraphs work together to convey meaning, including the logic and sequence of ideas   1   2   3   4
- **layout** including paragraphs and conventions associated with particular forms of writing   1   2   3   4
- **organisation** including the structure of written text, the order of paragraphs, and the chronology of plot   1   2   3   4
- **fiction, non-fiction and poetry** – the characteristic features of different genres   1   2   3   4

Critical evaluation of texts   **1   2   3   4**

You should:

- be able to evaluate the quality of texts   1   2   3   4
- be aware of how information and ideas are presented and can be interpreted in different ways, depending on point of view, context, purpose and audience   1   2   3   4

Technical terms   **1   2   3   4**

You should know and understand the terminology relating to:

- ▸ **word-level features**, for example: digraph; morpheme; phoneme; segment; suffix   1   2   3   4
- ▸ **sentence-level features**, for example: adverbial; clause; simple, compound and complex sentences; subject; word classes   1   2   3   4
- ▸ **text-level features**, for example: cohesion; figurative language; genre; plot; voice   1   2   3   4

Making sense of your perceived competence

Look back over your *perceived competence* grades. Note the most frequent response (the mode) within each area. Then record your overall mode – the most frequent response across *all* areas listed above.

mode

The nature and role of standard English

Knowledge at word level

Sentence level knowledge (grammar and punctuation)

Text level knowledge

Critical evaluation of texts

Technical terms

Overall

Mostly 1s Suggests that most competency expectations are exceeded. Your perceived competence would place you at the level of an English specialist. Well done!

Mostly 2s Suggests that most competency expectations are met comfortably. Some attention is necessary, however, in the weaker elements. Your perceived competence places you at a level about that of a non-English specialist. You probably have little to worry about.

Mostly 3s Suggests that *most* competency expectations are basically met, but further attention is necessary throughout. Your perceived competence places you at a level best described as *approaching* that specified for a non-English specialist.

Mostly 4s Suggests that most competency expectations are not met at present – at least, you don't think that they are! Don't worry about it just now – you have until the end of your training to catch up. Just make sure you do your homework in time.

Confidence

Consider carefully the areas included within the Programmes of Study for Key Stages 1 and 2 in the National Curriculum for English, as summarised below. Overall, how would you describe your confidence in terms of **teaching** these aspects of English? Please respond using the key provided.

1 = **Very good. Very confident – might even feel happy to support colleagues!**
2 = **Good. Might want to do a little revision before teaching.**
3 = **Adequate. Would need to do substantial revision before teaching this.**
4 = **Not good. Would need to work very hard to feel confident in teaching this.**

En1 Speaking and Listening

	1	2	3	4
• Speaking	1	2	3	4
• Listening	1	2	3	4
• Group discussion and interaction	1	2	3	4
• Drama	1	2	3	4
• Standard English	1	2	3	4
• Language variation	1	2	3	4

En2 Reading

	1	2	3	4
• Reading strategies	1	2	3	4
• Understanding texts (KS2 only)	1	2	3	4
• Reading for information	1	2	3	4
• Non-fiction and non-literary texts (KS2)	1	2	3	4
• Literature – fiction, poetry, drama	1	2	3	4
• Language structure and variation	1	2	3	4

En3 Writing

	1	2	3	4
• Composition	1	2	3	4
• Planning and drafting	1	2	3	4
• Punctuation	1	2	3	4
• Spelling	1	2	3	4
• Handwriting and presentation	1	2	3	4
• Standard English	1	2	3	4
• Language structure	1	2	3	4

Making sense of your perceived confidence

As before, if you've awarded yourself lots of 1s and 2s, that's brilliant! 3s are encouraging, and probably the commonest profile at this point in time. 4s? You've been brutally honest – and knowing what your weaknesses are is the first step to addressing them. Reflect critically on how confident you feel about teaching English and use the space below to comment further. Again, try to identify the source of your confidence or lack of it.

confidence statement

Part 4: English test

Your own perceptions about your competence and confidence in English subject knowledge might be quite different from how you would perform in a test. There may well be some areas with which you're unfamiliar, but probably also some which seem very easy.

A couple of points need to be clarified at the outset. Firstly, 'English' is not about knowing facts; it's about understanding how language is used. There is a great number of technical terms, and in order to describe and discuss language, knowing the names for these is important. Knowing names for their own sake is meaningless. Secondly, English is a fantastically rich and complex language, which is wonderful – but its complexity also means that it is full of potential for different interpretations, and hard and fast rules are few, while 'shades of grey' arise everywhere. For this reason, the test has been designed in a very simplistic manner, to enable a mainly right-or-wrong marking system which is straightforward for you to administer.

Because you are an expert user of English, with a huge amount of implicit knowledge about how language works, you will find that you can sometimes work out the answers using logic or by informed guesswork. To get the most out of using the test, you need to be tough on yourself and ask whether you could *explain* your correct answers to someone else. If you can't, plan some further revision!

Most sections of the test have been structured with a short True/False section to tune you in at the start, leading to more detailed questions which ask you to apply your knowledge and understanding within a particular area. Most sections then finish by refocusing on certain key elements of terminology, which gives you an opportunity to check your understanding and link back to preceding questions. There are areas of overlap between sections, English being the way it is!

The following pages explore your knowledge and understanding in many areas of primary English. Take as long as you need. As the test is long and quite intensive, you may prefer to tackle it section by section, checking your answers in Part 5 before you move on to the next part.

The nature and role of standard English

1 True or False?

(a) Standard English is spoken in certain parts of the British Isles only. _____
(b) Standard English is more commonly used in writing than in speaking. _____
(c) Standard English is the form of English most commonly used in formal situations. _____
(d) Standard English does not use local dialect forms. _____
(e) Standard English relates to grammar, vocabulary and spelling. _____
(f) Received Pronunciation is used when speaking in standard English. _____
(g) Standard English cannot be spoken in a regional accent. _____
(h) Foreigners learning English are likely to be taught standard English. _____
(i) People who are unable to use standard English can be disadvantaged. _____
(j) Standard English remains constant over time. _____

[10 MARKS]

2 In which of the following situations would you expect standard English to be most consistently used? Tick three.

(a) A written application for a teaching post. ☐

(b) Children talking in the playground. ☐

(c) A phone-in radio chat show. ☐

(d) The Chancellor's Budget speech. ☐

(e) A television news report. ☐

[3 MARKS]

3 Why might standard English be used in the situations ticked above? Tick two.

(a) It is informal. ☐

(b) It can be understood by a wide audience. ☐

(c) It identifies the user as an educated person who can use language appropriately. ☐

(d) It is pronounced in a non-regional accent. ☐

[2 MARKS]

4 Standard English or not standard English? Note SE or NSE.

(a) The children are seated on the carpet. _____

(b) I ain't got no money. _____

(c) May I order some drinks, please? _____

(d) You were about ten years old at the time. _____

(e) You better shove off, mate! _____

(f) Aghast, he looked at the twins. _____

[6 MARKS]

5 Dialect or accent – which is which?

(a) _____ offers clues about the speaker's origins through its choice of words and particular grammatical conventions.

(b) _____ refers to the way in which spoken language is pronounced, suggesting the speaker's geographical and/or social background.

[2 MARKS]

6 In the following sentences, circle attempts to represent **accent** through spelling, and underline any words which are features of **dialect**. In some sentences you will have examples of both.

(a) There's a crow on the chimley.

(b) I never promised you nowt.

(c) Look, I brung back yer key!

(d) Oi 'aven't seen 'im today.

(e) He's afeared.

(f) She's went oot.

(g) Stop blethering!

[7 MARKS]

11

The spoken and written language systems of English

All the sections that follow, dealing with knowledge at the levels of word, sentence and text, relate to both spoken and written English. However, before you tackle these, try this short section which looks directly at the relationship between speech and writing.

1 True or False?

(a) Both spoken and written language are produced with an audience in mind. _____

(b) Writing mirrors the structures of spoken language precisely. _____

(c) Spaces between words are a feature of written, rather than spoken, English. _____

(d) Written and spoken language can often serve the same purposes. _____

(e) Cohesion is a feature of spoken, rather than written, English. _____

(f) Bias only occurs in spoken English. _____

[6 MARKS]

2 Are the following extracts more likely to come from written language or (as transcripts) from spoken language?

(a) Hmm... OK, I'll see what I can come up with – hang on, got it! _____

(b) Private – trespassers will be prosecuted. _____

(c) Sorry, you can't come in, this is private woodland, like. _____

(d) See her over there? She gave me a real hard time, she did. _____

(e) Put it down there. _____

(f) The officer, who had been on leave at the time of the incident, declined to comment. _____

[6 MARKS]

3 Insert 'written' or 'spoken' as appropriate.

(a) Discrete sentences are found more commonly in _____ English.

(b) Regional variation is more commonly found in _____ English.

(c) _____ English tends to use more formal vocabulary and structures.

(d) In _____ English, the lack of context means that more explicit information needs to be provided.

(e) Complex sentences are more commonly found in _____ English.

(f) Grammatical structures are often less regular in _____ English.

(g) Language change tends to occur first in _____ English.

(h) _____ English provides a more permanent form of communication.

[8 MARKS]

Knowledge at word level

Phonics and how the writing system represents the sound system

1 True or False?

(a) Each letter in English corresponds to a single speech sound. _____
(b) The terms 'consonant' and 'vowel' refer to speech sounds. _____
(c) Some speech sounds can be spelled in more than one way. _____
(d) Phonemes vary from language to language. _____
(e) There are 33 phonemes in spoken English. _____

[5 MARKS]

2 Circle any two words that rhyme.

you   June   through   crew   cough   queue   view   my

[2 MARKS]

3 How many syllables are there in:

emu _____   hippopotamus _____

[2 MARKS]

4 Circle the onset and underline the rime.

seal   duck   owl

[3 MARKS]

5 How many phonemes are in each word?

lion _____   bear _____   jackal _____
elephant _____   ape _____

[5 MARKS]

6 Although spelled differently, each pair of words shares one common phoneme. Underline the letter(s) in each word that represent it.

zoo glasses   field key   rage just

[3 MARKS]

7 Underline any two letter groups representing adjacent consonant phonemes.

When her friend left, Flora felt so sad that she began to cry.

[2 MARKS]

8 Underline any two consonant digraphs in the list of words below.

elephant   gorilla   orang-utan   frog

[2 MARKS]

9 Underline any two vowel digraphs in the list of words below.

owl   chimpanzee   camel   ape

[2 MARKS]

10 Some words below contain trigraphs. Underline one consonant trigraph and circle one vowel trigraph.

catch   hold   edge   sigh

[2 MARKS]

11 caught   site   rain   grown   grey   kit   howl   mate   frown   toe   height

In the wordbank above, find a word which:

(a) rhymes with 'kite' but which spells the vowel phoneme differently;
(b) has the same initial and final phonemes as 'kite';
(c) includes the vowel phoneme found in 'crow', but spells it differently;
(d) includes the digraph 'ow' as in 'crow', but in which this is pronounced differently;
(e) has four phonemes;
(f) includes a split digraph.

[6 MARKS]

12 Identify two words in the list below which include a diphthong. Circle the corresponding letters.

howl   say   cat   sleep   boy   rabbit

[2 MARKS]

13 Circle the unstressed vowel grapheme (schwa) in the words.

grammar   sentence   misery

[3 MARKS]

14 Which of the following symbols, placed around a letter or letters, indicates that the reference is to the speech sound rather than the letters?

/a/ ☐   "a" ☐ |a| ☐   *a* ☐

[1 MARK]

15 Terminology

Fill in the blanks, using all but two of the words in the wordbank.

segment	syllable	digraph	onset	adjacent	reversible
trigraph	consonant	rime	phoneme	blend	grapheme

A _____ is the smallest contrastive unit of speech sound in a language.

In English, the letter or letters representing each speech sound in writing is called a _____ .
Where two letters represent a single speech sound, this is known as a _____ ; where three letters
are used, it is known as a _____ .

Each spoken word contains at least one _____ or beat. Each of these can be split into the
_____ (consonantal beginning) and the _____ (rhyming end part, containing the vowel).

When spelling a word, a writer first of all has to _____ the spoken word into its phonemes, and
then match to each of these a plausible letter representation. When using phonics to read a word,
a reader matches each letter (or group of letters) to a plausible speech sound, and goes on to
_____ the individual speech sounds together into a word. These processes are _____ .

[10 MARKS]

Morphology – word structure and derivations

1 True or False?

(a) Many English words have their origins in other languages. _____
(b) Knowing about word origins and relationships can help with spelling. _____
(c) Prefixes and suffixes can be added to the end of a word. _____
(d) Morphemes are double-length phonemes. _____
(e) Many common English words are derived from Anglo-Saxon. _____

[5 MARKS]

2 Identify four compound words in the following list:

beheaded	arrowhead	headlight	redhead
header	heading	headteacher	headless

[4 MARKS]

3 Many words in the English vocabulary suggest clues as to their origins in classical languages. Draw lines to match the following words to their language of origin.

psychology		alphabet
submarine	Latin	century
phoneme		grammar
innate	Greek	circumnavigate

[8 MARKS]

4 The English language has imported words from many other languages. Match the words that follow to their language of origin, choosing from the wordbank below. Note: you will not need to use all the languages. As you make your decisions, reflect on your reasons for doing so.

Gaelic   French   Greek   Hindi   German   Finnish
Afrikaans   Spanish   Arabic   Italian

sauna _____   whisky _____
mutton _____   algebra _____
apartheid _____   kindergarten _____
potato _____   shampoo _____

[8 MARKS]

5 Separate the following words into prefix, root (or base form) and suffix, as appropriate:

	Prefix	Root	Suffix
(a) unwrapping	_____	_____	_____
(b) precede	_____	_____	_____
(c) strangeness	_____	_____	_____
(d) subtraction	_____	_____	_____

[4 MARKS]

6 Underline the prefixes in the following words and draw lines to match them to their meanings. *Note: you will have one meaning left over.*

(a) extrasensory   not

(b) dishonest   within
                          before
(c) intravenous   outside

(d) international   between

[4 MARKS]

16

7   The words in bold type in the sentence below have inflectional suffixes to enable them to carry out their grammatical function in the sentence.

When the **results** were announced, Kate **scored** a **higher** mark than Rob. However, **Jason's** score was the **highest** of all.

Underline the inflectional suffix **only** in each word below (be precise!) and draw lines to match suffixes to functions. You will have one function left over.

(a) results

(b) Jason's

(c) highest

(d) scored

(e) higher

comparative adjective

superlative adjective

possessive form of plural noun

plural noun

past tense verb

possessive form of singular noun

[5 MARKS]

(½ each for identifying the inflection, ½ each for matching to its function)

8   From the words given, create a new word, in the specified word class, by adding a derivational suffix (you may need to make spelling changes in some cases).

(a) A noun from **rigid**.   _____

(b) A noun from **good**.   _____

(c) A verb from **bright**.   _____

(d) An adjective from **energy**.   _____

(e) An adverb from **rapid**.   _____

[5 MARKS]

9   Terminology

Use the following wordbank to fill in the blanks. You will have two words left over.

morphology   root   aspiration   prefix   inflection

suffix   etymology   compound word   morpheme

Within _____ , which means the study of word structure, the smallest unit of meaning in a word is known as a _____ . The core unit of meaning in any word is called its _____ . This may form the complete word, such as **dog**. Sometimes two such elements are joined to create a longer _____ , like **sheepdog**.

Words can be extended by adding extra elements of meaning. If a _____ is added at the start of a word a new word is created, such as **in + form = inform**. A _____ is added at the end of a word; this can also create a new word, such as **form + al**. However, often it performs a grammatical function, enabling a word to carry out its job within a sentence, as in **form + ed = formed**, when it is known as an _____ .

[7 MARKS]

Word meanings and how words relate to each other

1   True or False?

(a) In English, there are often several words or expressions that mean much the same thing. _____

(b) Words which are pronounced the same are always spelled the same. _____

(c) Speakers select the words they use depending on the situation and the person they are addressing. _____

(d) Colloquial language means the same as slang. _____

(e) Some words have kept their spelling but changed their pronunciation over the years. _____

[5 MARKS]

2   From the sentences below, identify two words that are:

(a) homographs   _____   _____

(b) homophones   _____   _____

(c) synonyms   _____   _____

(d) antonyms   _____   _____

- I need new brake blocks for my bike.
- He had to rush to catch the train.
- We had a furious row.
- What a tiny puppy!
- Don't break the seal.
- Let's sit in the front row.
- Let's hurry.
- My dad grew some enormous potatoes this year!

[8 MARKS]

3   In the list below, underline six words that can have quite different meanings depending on the context in which they are used, despite looking and sounding the same. For example, *ball* could mean something to throw, or a dance.

cross	interesting	and	plant	play	happiness
shoot	towards	foot	politician	tomato	cricket

[6 MARKS]

4   Words can have meanings which are similar but not identical. Sort the following words by meaning into three groups (label A, B, C):

pretty	lively	handsome	intelligent	energetic
active	bright	beautiful	clever	quick-witted

[3 MARKS]

5 Order the following words on a scale of intensity, from least to most:

(a) (temperature)   cold   warm   hot   freezing   tepid

_____

(b) (volume)   call   say   shout   whisper   mutter

_____

[2 MARKS]

6 Some common words originated as abbreviations of longer words. Which three words are abbreviated, and from what?

park   pram   coal   zoo   gum   vet

_____   _____   _____

[3 MARKS]

7 Circle six sentences or phrases which would not be classed as standard English expressions, but as colloquialisms or slang.

Thank you.   I'm hard up.   I have no money.   I am sleepy.

I'm skint.   Be quiet.   I need some kip.   Shut up!

Please help.   Let's go for a meal!   Let's chill out.   I'm broke.

[6 MARKS]

8 Note any three expressions from the above list which have a similar meaning.

_____   _____   _____

[3 MARKS]

9 The following extract from a telephone conversation contains a number of non-standard English expressions. Identify these and replace, using standard English:

Gemma: Hi, Gemma here.

Sara: It's Sara. Just thought I'd give you a buzz to get the low-down on Pete and Gill.

Gemma: Hang on a mo – I'll just switch the telly off.

[6 MARKS]

10 Adapt the vocabulary in the following sentence so that a young child could understand it.

It is essential that you desist from weeping immediately.

[1 MARK]

Ⓣ **11** **Terminology**

Match each word to its meaning. You will have one word left over.

synonym	(a) word with same spelling as another but different meaning
colloquialism	(b) word with opposite meaning to another
acronym	(c) word formed from initial letters or syllables of other words
homonym	(d) word with similar meaning to another
homograph	(e) word with same spelling or sound as another but with a
abbreviation	different meaning or origin
antonym	(f) word with same sound as another but different meaning or spelling
homophone	(g) form of expression used in familiar talk

[7 MARKS]

Sentence level knowledge – grammar and punctuation

Word classes and cohesion within a sentence

1 True or False?

(a) Every word belongs to one particular class (part of speech). ⎯⎯⎯

(b) Word class depends on a word's current function in a sentence. ⎯⎯⎯

(c) All words in a sentence are essential to convey meaning. ⎯⎯⎯

(d) Cohesion refers to the grammatical features in a sentence or text which
bind it together to make linguistic sense. ⎯⎯⎯

(e) Where a sentence lacks cohesion, it is harder to understand. ⎯⎯⎯

[5 MARKS]

2 After reading the following text, identify examples of the word classes listed below. Select the clearest (most obvious) examples you can.

Following the play, which was extremely enjoyable, Charles and Jo went for a meal to a well-known local restaurant, where, to their surprise, they found other diners included members of the cast. To Jo's delight, Peter Robbins, the leading man, was sitting at the next table to theirs.

(a)	proper noun	⎯⎯⎯⎯	(g)	pronoun	⎯⎯⎯⎯
(b)	abstract noun	⎯⎯⎯⎯	(h)	preposition	⎯⎯⎯⎯
(c)	concrete noun	⎯⎯⎯⎯	(i)	conjunction	⎯⎯⎯⎯
(d)	collective noun	⎯⎯⎯⎯	(j)	determiner	⎯⎯⎯⎯
(e)	verb	⎯⎯⎯⎯	(k)	adjective	⎯⎯⎯⎯
(f)	adverb	⎯⎯⎯⎯	(l)	relative pronoun	⎯⎯⎯⎯

[12 MARKS]

3 In what person is the above extract written?

1st? ☐   2nd? ☐   3rd? ☐

[1 MARK]

4   If **Jo** were telling the tale, which word class would need to change?

    (a) pronouns ☐

    (b) prepositions ☐

    (c) adjectives ☐

[1 MARK]

5   In what tense is the above extract written?

    Past ☐   Present ☐   Future ☐

[1 MARK]

6   When you condense a message to its bare essentials, as below, which are the **main** word classes you usually need to retain?

Want teddy.   **Gone fishing.**   **Tea in fridge.**   **Man hiccups for three weeks!**

    (a) pronouns, prepositions ☐

    (b) nouns, verbs ☐

    (c) adverbs, adjectives ☐

[1 MARK]

7   Verbs can consist of more than one word, when they are known as verb chains. The main verb carries the meaning, while one or more auxiliary verbs help it express that meaning in a particular context. Underline the verb chains in the following sentences. Then identify the main and auxiliary verbs which make up each verb chain.

	Main verb form	Auxiliary verb(s)
(a) I am going to the library now.	_____	_____
(b) I will have finished my test by midnight.	_____	_____
(c) May I go home?	_____	_____

[6 MARKS]

(3 for identifying verb chains, 3 for splitting into main and auxiliary verbs)

8   Verbs can be finite or non-finite. Tick the status of the underlined verb in the following sentences:

    (a) I would like to <u>know</u> what a finite verb is!   finite ☐   non-finite ☐

    (b) He <u>likes</u> chocolate.   finite ☐   non-finite ☐

    (c) <u>Are</u> you over 21?   finite ☐   non-finite ☐

[3 MARKS]

21

9 Circle one noun phrase and underline one prepositional phrase.

the white horse	went home	after the famous hurricane
is helping out	my mum	the boy carrying the suitcase

[2 MARKS]

10 Words can belong to different classes depending on their role in a sentence.

Example: My home is in Norfolk.   Home is a noun in this context.
I went home.   Home is an adverb in this context.

Identify the word class of the underlined word in each sentence, choosing from the following list. You may need to use some words more than once, and others not at all.

noun   verb   determiner   adjective   adverb   preposition   conjunction

(a) Please <u>dress</u> very quickly.   _____

(b) She was wearing a short red <u>dress</u>.   _____

(c) I ate a succulent <u>orange</u>.   _____

(d) Would <u>orange</u> paint look right?   _____

(e) He went <u>inside</u>.   _____

(f) Please leave it <u>inside</u> the porch.   _____

[6 MARKS]

11 Alter this sentence by substituting two more powerful verbs, for example, to add clarity, precision or impact.

'Get out of my way,' she said, and went out of the room in a bad temper.

[2 MARKS]

12 Expand the noun phrase in this sentence to provide more information.

I have a dog which is very friendly.

[1 MARK]

13 Change **all** singular references to plural in this sentence.

That man is eating my pizza.

[1 MARK]

14 Identify the 'problem' in each of the following sentences which gives rise to a loss of cohesion. Also select an appropriate remedy for each.

(i) Miss Hayes was cross with Jenny because she was in a bad mood.

(ii) All the clothes was lying in a big heap.

(iii) I asked mum if I can go to the shops and she says yes.

(iv) I think grey squirrels are a nuisance, because grey squirrels eat the birds' food.

Problem: sentence number:

(a) ambiguity   _____
(b) repetition   _____
(c) inconsistent tense   _____
(d) lack of subject-verb agreement   _____

Remedies:

(e) use pronoun instead of phrase   _____
(f) alter verb tense   _____
(g) alter verb form   _____
(h) clarify referent of pronoun   _____

[8 MARKS]

15 Terminology
Circle the correct alternative.

(a) A **verb/noun/adjective** is a word which names a person, place or thing.
(b) Most nouns can be preceded by a **preposition/determiner/pronoun**.
(c) **Most conjunctions/nouns/adjectives** can take a singular or plural form.
(d) **Adverbs/verbs/conjunctions** refer to what is happening in a sentence.
(e) **Verbs/adverbs/determiners** can be written in the present or past tense.
(f) **Adverbs/conjunctions/prepositions** link words, phrases or clauses.
(g) A **pronoun/adjective/adverb** provides more information about a noun.
(h) A **pronoun/adjective/adverb** stands in place of a noun.
(i) An **adjective/adverb/preposition** gives more information about a verb.
(j) A word that indicates a relationship, often standing at the head of a phrase, such as 'in the house',
    is a **determiner/preposition/adjective**.

[10 MARKS]

Sentence types and structure

1 True or False?

(a) Sentences always express a statement.   _____
(b) Sentences need to stand alone and make sense.   _____
(c) Complex sentences can be shorter than simple sentences.   _____
(d) Sentences cannot have only one clause.   _____
(e) Local dialects never include non-standard grammatical structures. _____

[5 MARKS]

2 Are the following sentences examples of a question, exclamation, command or statement?
Be careful – punctuation is not always a straightforward clue.

(a) Which age group do you prefer?   _____
(b) I prefer teaching at Key Stage 1.   _____
(c) Will you pay attention?   _____
(d) Plan your lessons more carefully.   _____
(e) I just can't believe your test scores! _____

[5 MARKS]

3 Change the following question to the other sentence types specified.

Have you eaten the last biscuit?

(a) **Command:** _____

(b) **Statement:** _____

[2 MARKS]

4 Label: phrase or clause?

(a) **after the test** _____

(b) **a long, complicated test** _____

(c) **when I have finished the test** _____

(d) **with an enormous yawn** _____

[4 MARKS]

5 Label the subject and predicate.

The older children were studying algebra.

[2 MARKS]

6 Label the subject, verb and object.

The older children were studying algebra.

[3 MARKS]

7 Label the subject, verb, object and adverbial.

As quickly as possible, Ms Peters dismissed the class.

[4 MARKS]

8 Rewrite the sentence in Question 7, replacing the subject by a subject of your own choice.

_____

[1 MARK]

9 Rewrite the sentence in Question 7, moving the adverbial to a different slot in the sentence.

_____

[1 MARK]

10 Insert appropriate verbs into the following sentence so it makes sense.

Mr Sharp (a) _____ **down, (b)** _____ **his briefcase and (c)** _____ **a file to the Inspector.**

Which of the inserted verbs are transitive? _____

Which are intransitive? _____

[2 MARKS]

11 Identify three sentences below which use the passive voice.

(a) My car was damaged by vandals.
(b) We have finished drinking beer.
(c) Tonight's flight has been delayed by bad weather.
(d) All the beer has been drunk now.
(e) Some vandals damaged my car.
(f) The bad weather has delayed tonight's flight.

[3 MARKS]

12 Underline the main clause and circle the subordinate clause in the sentences below.

(a) Freddie, who had rather enjoyed the free wine, felt frivolous.
(b) After I finish writing up my assignment, I'm going to watch a horror film.
(c) Cordelia has not done her homework because she left her notebook in school.

[6 MARKS]

13 Identify the following as simple, compound or complex sentences:

(a) Joe, when he had finished his essay, volunteered to wash up.   _____
(b) Joe washed up although it was not his turn.   _____
(c) Joe washed up yesterday, after tea.   _____
(d) Joe finished his essay, had tea and washed up.   _____

Which of the above sentences includes an embedded clause?   _____

[5 MARKS]

14 Coordinating or subordinating conjunctions? Write C or S against them.

and ____   when ____   although ____   if ____   or ____

[5 MARKS]

15 The following complex sentence contains three subordinating conjunctions. Underline them.

If you apply for a teaching post while you are still a trainee, you have every chance of success. Because you have not yet attained NQT status, however, any appointment must remain provisional.

[3 MARKS]

16 Some of the following sentences include a clause headed by a relative pronoun. Circle three relative pronouns.

My sister, because she is a teacher, works long hours.
My sister, whose children are still very young, is taking a career break.
My sister, who lives in Norfolk, has a cat which is scared of mice.

[3 MARKS]

ⓣ **17** Terminology

Match the descriptions to terms from the respective wordbank. You will have one extra term on each occasion.

predicate   adverbial   subject   object

(a) _____   identifies what or who the sentence is about
(b) _____   tells what the subject does, or is; contains the action of the sentence
(c) _____   identifies who or what is affected by the subject's action

standard sentence   compound sentence   simple sentence   complex sentence

(d) _____   consists of one clause
(e) _____   contains two or more main clauses
(f) _____   contains main clause and one or more subordinate clauses

[6 MARKS]

Punctuation

1 True or False?

(a) Word spacing is a feature of spoken, rather than written, English.   _____
(b) Punctuation conventions have changed over time.   _____
(c) Intonation and gesture replace punctuation in spoken English.   _____
(d) Punctuation mainly clarifies grammatical structure and thus meaning.   _____
(e) Punctuation mainly indicates where to take a breath when speaking.   _____

[5 MARKS]

2 Rewrite the following sentences, inserting all necessary punctuation.

(a) he brought me a bar of chocolate some crisps and a bottle of white wine
(b) go and apologise said mrs taylor and offer to help tidy up
(c) christopher who had finished his lunch by ten o clock had nothing left to eat
(d) mum help cried sally
(e) although the war ended in 1945 its repercussions were felt for a very long time afterwards

[10 MARKS]

(2 for each completely correct sentence, 1 if only one error is made in a sentence)

3 Correct one common punctuational error in each of the following sentences:

(a) After lunch, we went to the park, it was deserted.
(b) 'Mum can we go out to play now?' asked Rosie.
(c) We had sausage's and roast potatoes.
(d) No!. That can't be true!
(e) Becky's cat was licking it's kittens.

[5 MARKS]

4 Which of the three alternatives is correct?

(a) 'Tonight,' suggested George, 'Let's go to the theatre.' ☐
(b) 'Tonight, suggested George, let's go to the theatre.' ☐
(c) 'Tonight,' suggested George, 'let's go to the theatre.' ☐

[1 MARK]

5 Rewrite the following sentences, changing the punctuation **only** to substantially alter the meaning. Do not change the word order or alter any words.

(a) After he had eaten, my dog Sam was violently sick on the carpet.
(b) If you're unsure – don't! Ask me what to do.
(c) The teacher punished the boys. For no good reason, they told their parents.
(d) Trolls usually smell nasty. Children are afraid of them.

[4 MARKS]

6 Terminology
Match the common punctuation marks below to their function within a sentence. You will have one punctuation mark left over. Note: some also have other functions which are not listed here.

apostrophe
semi-colon
dash
full stop
exclamation mark
comma

(a) marks grammatical boundaries within a sentence
(b) adds emphasis, volume or emotion at the end of a sentence
(c) signals the end of a sentence (usually a statement)
(d) indicates possession or omission of letters
(e) links closely related statements

[5 MARKS]

Textual knowledge

Cohesion, layout and organisation

1 True or False?

(a) Speakers and writers tailor their use of language to suit their purpose and audience. _____
(b) Without cohesion, a text is likely to be less coherent. _____
(c) All texts are organised with a beginning, middle and end. _____
(d) Certain textual conventions and structures are mainly found in written English. _____
(e) Meaning and layout are unrelated. _____

[5 MARKS]

2   Sequence the following paragraphs from a guidebook into a cohesive text – one that makes linguistic sense.

(a) Its position in an area of natural beauty, just north of Butser Hill, ensures that it maintains a completely separate identity from the Portsmouth conurbation to the south.

(b) The square also provides access to the much-visited Norman church, and opens on to Sheep Street where some of the town's oldest houses can be found. These date from the 16th century.

(c) Petersfield is a small town in East Hampshire.

(d) This enables it to retain its traditional market-town character. Sadly, however, agricultural markets no longer take place in the historic town square around the central statue of William III.

(e) In contrast, on the opposite side of the square is the recently completed Rams Walk shopping centre. This has helped the town remain a popular destination.

[5 MARKS]

3   Connectives and pronouns contribute to textual cohesion. Circle three connectives and underline three pronouns in the text above. These may have helped you sequence the text.

[6 MARKS]

4   A 9-year-old boy wrote the following text, which lacks cohesion in certain respects. Alter three words to remedy some common errors, specifically improving cohesion.

Tom opened the heavy, iron gate and Tom saw something incredible – a tropical beach! The sun was golden, like a red-hot fireball, and the sea is gleaming like a million sapphire jewels. It was out of this world! Tom decided to walk along the sandy shore. Suddenly I saw a little golden key in the sand, and picked it up.

[3 MARKS]

5   The way in which texts are physically laid out varies according to their purpose.

Tick all the text forms which tend to follow a fairly conventional layout (one that you would instantly recognise).

newspaper article ☐   restaurant menu ☐   playscript ☐

formal business letter ☐   telephone directory ☐   dictionary ☐

[1 MARK]

6   Why is textual layout important in relation to meaning? Tick four statements:

(a) It can chop a text into coherent chunks that are easier to read.   ☐

(b) It can indicate the theme of a story.   ☐

(c) It can help you to locate information easily.   ☐

(d) It can draw your attention rapidly to the main idea of the text.   ☐

(e) It can usually help you work out what individual words mean.   ☐

(f) It can often give an instant idea of the kind of text you are dealing with.   ☐

[4 MARKS]

7 The following extracts originally contained three paragraphs each. Mark where you think each paragraph should begin.

(i) 'You'd better go and get us something to eat,' said Charlie. 'I'll wait here until you get back, just in case Jenny arrives in the meantime.' 'OK – what do you want? Pizza again?' 'Sounds good,' said Charlie. He licked his lips. 'Make mine a cheese and tomato, extra large – I'm starving.'

(ii) The Primary National Strategy *Framework for Literacy* was published in Autumn 2006. This was designed to integrate existing documentation into a single coherent framework and increase manageability for teachers. Additionally, driven by a continuing drive to raise standards, it was intended to create a renewed sense of momentum in literacy teaching. Organisationally, the *Framework* is divided into twelve strands of learning objectives which relate to the Early Learning Goals for the Foundation Stage and to the National Curriculum for Key Stages 1 and 2. The objectives are ordered by year to promote systematic progression within each strand. The innovative electronic publication of the *Framework* offers a number of advantages over the previous print version. For example, direct hyperlinks to associated guidance and resources enable teachers to access specific resources as appropriate for their needs. The electronic format also enables rapid updating of materials.

[4 MARKS]

(no marks for getting the start of the first paragraph right!)

8 Select from the list below one function of the paragraphing in the texts above:

(a) to clarify who is speaking
(b) to mark a change of time or setting
(c) to indicate how to read the text aloud
(d) to mark a change of focus

Text (i) _____   Text (ii) _____

[2 MARKS]

Fiction, non-fiction and poetry

1 True or False?

(a) Most people, in daily life, read more fiction than non-fiction.   _____
(b) Electronic texts cannot be considered as non-fiction.   _____
(c) Reference books, like fiction, have to be read from beginning to end.   _____
(d) Non-fiction texts tend to use impersonal language, which children
      can find more difficult.   _____
(e) Different types of text are organised differently.   _____

[5 MARKS]

2 Fiction, poetry or non-fiction? Mark F, P or NF against the following titles:

(a) Ode to a Nightingale   _____
(b) A Culinary Tour of Scotland   _____
(c) San Diego Zoo website   _____
(d) The Wind in the Willows   _____

[4 MARKS]

29

3 Many stories are structured according to a basic pattern. In the following chronological summary of the *Cinderella* story, match events to the terms listed below:

development   problem   resolution   orientation   ending   climax

(a) Cinderella lives miserably with her lazy, ugly sisters.   _____
(b) The two sisters go to the ball, leaving Cinderella at home,
    wishing she too could go.   _____
(c) The Fairy Godmother arrives, and grants Cinderella's wish.
    Cinderella attends the ball; the prince falls madly in love
    with her.   _____
(d) Midnight – as the magic runs out, Cinderella has to leave (but
    drops a slipper).   _____
(e) The Prince finds the slipper fits Cinderella.   _____
(f) Wedding bells!   _____

[6 MARKS]

4 Below are listed several fictional genres which commonly feature in the primary school, and a list of statements suggesting some typical generic features relating to characters, plot, setting or language. Which genres best match the descriptions? Note you will have two genres left over.

fable   adventure story   historical fiction   science fiction
        legend   fairy tale   myth   horror story

(a) Usually includes animal characters who talk and act
    like humans; short, intended to teach a moral lesson.   _____
(b) Setting located in the defined past; vocabulary may
    reflect this; may merge with other genres such as
    adventure or romance.   _____
(c) Ancient traditional story of heroes and gods, tackles a
    concern of human existence; may explain some
    natural phenomenon.   _____
(d) Plot involves realistic characters engaging in and overcoming
    a series of exciting, often hazardous events.   _____
(e) Traditional tale, often rooted in historical fact, which describes
    the actions of a hero figure.   _____
(f) Includes stereotypical characters, whose lives are affected in
    some way by magic; often highly predictable.   _____

[6 MARKS]

5 Match each story opening to the 'best fit' genre, choosing from the list above:

(i) Once upon a time, in a tumbledown cottage in a deep dark wood, there lived two poor sisters. Marguerite was fair and gentle, loved far and wide for her kind and thoughtful ways. Violet was dark and quick-tempered, with black eyes that flashed scornfully at all who displeased her.

Genre: _____

(ii) I never knew my father, who was cut down at Culloden in '46, fighting for the royal cause. He died nobly, one amongst thousands of brave Scots who lost their lives striking a futile blow for freedom, leaving my mother alone to raise four hungry children.

Genre: _____

(iii) Once there was a greedy fox who invited his neighbour Rabbit round for a slap-up dinner. More fool Rabbit for agreeing to go, I say – after all, everyone knows foxes are crafty critters who can't think further ahead than their next meal!

Genre: _____

[3 MARKS]

6 Note one of the extracts above in which:

(a) the voice is that of a character in the story _____

(b) the voice is that of the author, as an impersonal narrator _____

(c) the story is set in a defined place and time _____

(d) the characters are stereotyped _____

(e) the plot is more or less predictable _____

(f) the style is colloquial. _____

[6 MARKS]

7 Non-fiction text types

At Key Stages 1 and 2, children typically become familiar with the following: **recount, explanation, persuasive text, discussion, instructions** and **non-chronological report**.

Which three are characterised by the following textual structure?

(a) opening statement of issue, series of ordered arguments
for and against issue, conclusion _____

(b) opening to set the scene, outline of events in chronological
order, closing statement _____

(c) general opening statement, leading to more detailed
factual description of phenomena _____

[3 MARKS]

8 Organise the following list into an appropriate planning structure for a **persuasive argument** by numbering them in an appropriate order below.

(a) It costs a lot more to feed a cheetah than a corgi.

(b) Cheetahs need an enormous amount of exercise, much more than a corgi.

(c) Taking everything into account, I suggest you buy a corgi.

(d) In my opinion, although a cheetah sounds more exciting, it appears to have few advantages.

(e) I know you're considering buying a cheetah or a corgi.

(f) Cheetahs are harder to train.

Structure: _____

[2 MARKS]

9 Identify the 'best fit' text type for the following four extracts. Choose from this list:

recount, explanation, persuasive text, discussion, instructions, non-chronological report.

(i) In order to land, a bird first raises its tail to steer it downwards. It then brakes by bringing its body upright, thus tilting its wings to the vertical to create wind resistance. It then lowers its tail. The bird's strong leg muscles absorb the impact of landing.

Text type: _____

(ii) First, decide on the position, size and shape of your pond. Mark out the edges and dig. When the hole is deep enough, line it with sand. Next, carefully position the rubber liner and add a layer of soil. Fill up with water. Finally, cover the liner edges.

Text type: _____

(iii) Later, went with Hayes to the Gaiety to see Macbeth – in my view, the most powerful play ever written. Afterwards enjoyed a quick tipple in the Five Jackdaws.

Text type: _____

[3 MARKS]

10 Which text(s) above demonstrate the following features?

(a) impersonal style _____
(b) connectives of time _____
(c) causal connectives _____
(d) imperative present tense verb _____
(e) past tense verbs _____

[5 MARKS]

11 Primary children are expected to become familiar with a range of poetry forms. In each question below, circle the poetry form which best matches the description that follows. This may relate to content or structure.

(a) A **narrative poem/sonnet/haiku** is a poem which tells a story.
(b) Poetry which follows a metrical pattern, but does not rhyme, is known as **blank verse/free verse/limerick**.
(c) A **calligram/limerick/rap** is a comic poem with five lines, following an **aabba** rhyme scheme and a set syllabic pattern.
(d) In a **haiku/rap/calligram**, the way in which the poem is physically printed and laid out on the page relates to what it is about.
(e) A **sonnet/narrative poem/haiku** has three lines, comprising 5, 7 and 5 syllables respectively.

[5 MARKS]

12 The first locomotive, *by Matthew (aged 11):*

I see a great green dragon,
A metal monster,
Hurtling forwards like a lightning bolt,
Hissing and spitting out sparks of hell,
Like a demon breathing out fire,
Clanging and banging,
Crashing and flashing,
Tearing along a steel track,
Like a madman,
Then screeching and screaming wildly
To a stop.
Silence.

Note one way in which this poem would differ from a prose account of the same experience.

_____

_____

[1 MARK]

13 Mark and label one example of each of the following poetic devices in the poem above.

simile   metaphor   alliteration   onomatopoeia   internal rhyme   assonance
[6 MARKS]

14 Terminology in fiction
Insert one word from the wordbank into each blank. You will have one word left over.

plot   theme   viewpoint   resolution   style   voice

Stories are essentially recounts of events. The _____ is the chronological sequence which links events causally. A story may also have a deeper underlying meaning (such as the triumph of good over evil), which is its _____ .

The *way* in which a story is written is important. The author may tell it through his or her _____, as an unspecified outsider who knows absolutely everything. Alternatively, it may be related from the particular _____ of a participant in the story. In this case, the _____ of writing may be more personal, reflecting the type of language used by that particular person.
[5 MARKS]

15 Terminology in poetry and fiction (figurative language)
Circle the correct alternative:

(a) **Onomatopoeia/alliteration/simile** refers to a phrase in which words begin with the same phoneme.
(b) **Onomatopoeia/metaphor/personification** refers to the effect created by words whose sound echoes their meaning.

33

(c) **Simile/metaphor/repetition** refers to an author describing something as if it is something else.

(d) **Metaphor/personification/simile** refers to an author describing something non-human as if it has human qualities.

[4 MARKS]

Ⓣ **16** Terminology in non-fiction

Texts, or parts of texts, can be classified according to their purposes. Primary children typically become familiar with the following types of non-fiction text: **recount, explanation, persuasive text, discussion, instructions** and **non-chronological report**.

Match the above six text types to their purposes:

(a) describe arguments from different viewpoints, leading to a balanced conclusion

(b) explain how or why something occurs

(c) retell series of events, to entertain or inform

(d) tell reader what to do

(e) provide a factual description of something

(f) argue the case for a particular point of view

_____
_____
_____
_____
_____
_____

[6 MARKS]

Critical evaluation of texts

Evaluating the quality of texts

It is important to feel confident in evaluating the quality of texts, as you need to know exactly what to look out for when selecting a text to use for teaching. Evaluating text quality as such involves a high degree of subjectivity, and is impossible to test; but you can certainly make a start on selecting 'good books' to use in teaching by considering some general criteria. Clearly you need to look for different features in different types of text, as these tasks will demonstrate.

Note: 'exceptions' will always occur, so go for the 'best fit' option.

1 Listed below are some possible criteria which would help with the selection of 'good books'. Which types of book might the various criteria apply to? Choose from:

- reference book (non-fiction) for any age   R
- picture story book for beginning readers (age 4–6)   P
- historical novel for readers aged 7–11   H

(a) _____ Information is up to date and accurate.
(b) _____ Readers find the content interesting.
(c) _____ The illustrations help the reader to understand the words.
(d) _____ The plot is coherent and gripping.
(e) _____ The text uses a variety of sentence structures.

(f)	_____	The reader can relate to characters and their dilemmas.
(g)	_____	The author constructs and develops character through the use of dialogue, action and/or description.
(h)	_____	The language uses natural language structures and rhythms.
(i)	_____	The book is organised to help you find the information you want.
(j)	_____	The language is often patterned and predictable.
(k)	_____	The print is very clear and quite large.
(l)	_____	Specialist vocabulary is explained in a comprehensive glossary.
(m)	_____	Incidents in the text raise issues.
(n)	_____	The opening really makes you want to find out what happens next.
(o)	_____	Information about the setting in time is skilfully woven into the main text.

[15 MARKS MAXIMUM]

(1 for one [or more] acceptable answers against each statement)

2 And now, having considered the positive, what **critical** comments might you make about the following extracts? Note your comments beside each piece of text, aiming for at least ten in total, one or more per text.

(a) **My cat** (poem for KS1)

My cat came in the kitchen
While we were making tea.
I poured her a bowl of milk
And poured some more for me!

(b) Instructions (KS1/ KS2)

How to make coffee
Do you like coffee? Lots of people like coffee. This is how you make coffee. You pour boiling water into a cup with instant coffee in. Then you add sugar and milk.

(c) Early reading book (KS1)

Mum came in.
Dad came in.
Mum was cross.
Dad was cross.
Mum said Where is that cat?
She has been a bad cat today.

(d) Novel (Year 5/6)

The two-headed, hammer-tailed lizard dwelt in the stagnant, miry heart of the swamp known as Hell-hole, emerging only in the midst of nights black as thunder and wild as dragons to lurk unseen and unimagined by the rocky track to the mountain temple, alert and ravenous, intending to snatch and savour an unsuspecting nocturnal pilgrim. He was to bring back his head before sunrise.

(e) Non-fiction (KS2)

The largest country in the world is the USSR (or Soviet Union). It comprises a number of republics, including Armenia, Russia, Georgia and Lithuania. The capital city is Kiev.

[1 MARK per comment – to maximum of 10]

An awareness of how information and ideas are presented and can be interpreted in different ways, depending on point of view, context, purpose and audience

1 Consider the following four texts on the same subject, but in different contexts, written by a class teacher.

(i) Listen to the middle sound and write a letter for it.
(ii) Although Simon can now segment spoken words into phonemes, he remains insecure in representing medial vowel phonemes, especially digraphs, in writing.
(iii) 14/4/01 Several MVs in unaided work – bus, tran (train), grat (great).
(iv) Simon's doing brilliantly! He can now hear beginning and end sounds and write letters for them. He needs to work at middle sounds next.

Now match the text number to audience and purpose:

Audience		**Purpose**	
a) Simon's parents	_____	e) to inform a specialist	_____
b) Simon	_____	f) to make personal notes	_____
c) psychologist	_____	g) to inform child of his target	_____
d) teacher herself	_____	h) to inform parents	_____

[8 MARKS]

2 Which of the following textual features provided the clues that helped you to make the above decisions? Tick four:

(a) sentence construction ☐   (e) use of passive voice ☐
(b) complexity of vocabulary ☐   (f) use of determiners ☐
(c) layout ☐   (g) formal/informal style ☐
(d) person ☐   (h) specialist terminology ☐

[4 MARKS]

3 Are the following statements presented as fact or opinion?

(a) The first National Curriculum was introduced in 1989. _____
(b) Schools have a legal responsibility to teach the National Curriculum. _____

(c) It is vital that children learn to punctuate accurately. _____

(d) Literacy has improved, but at the expense of creativity. _____

[4 POINTS]

4 Which of each sentence pair expresses the speaker's or writer's particular slant on events?

(i) 'I have not marked 5F's books yet,' said Ms Fisher. ☐

(ii) '5F's books have not been marked yet,' said Ms Fisher. ☐

(iii) 'Some trains on the London line have been delayed due to a fallen tree on the line.' ☐

(iv) 'The trains have been delayed *again*!' ☐

(v) Despite being blessed with Madonna's acting talents, this film bombed. ☐

(vi) This film, which starred Madonna, was not a box-office success. ☐

[3 MARKS]

5 In the **ticked** sentences above, how have the authors or speakers adapted their use of language to express their own preferred versions of events? Match the descriptions that follow to the **ticked** sentences above.

(a) passive voice used in order to mask responsibility _____

(b) choice of vocabulary _____

(c) selective omission of details _____

(d) intonation used to emphasise viewpoint _____

[4 MARKS]

6 Fact: When the whistle blew, the score was Southampton 2, Liverpool 1.

(a) Write a news headline from a Southampton supporter's point of view.

_____

(b) Write a news headline from a Liverpool supporter's point of view.

_____

[2 MARKS]

Terminology

The real test of whether you understand the technical terminology used in English is whether you can use it. In this respect, the whole test has really put your understanding of the terminology through its paces. However, if you want to give yourself a score specifically in this area, simply add up your marks from all the Terminology questions (indicated by a ⓣ) at the end of each section (maximum of 60 marks).

Making sense of your test results

How well did you do?

Note down your scores and percentages for individual sections of the test. You can now compare how you scored in *each individual area* of English.

Area of English	Maximum possible	Your raw score	Your percentage score
The nature and role of standard English	30	____	____
The spoken and written language systems of English	20	____	____
Word-level knowledge			
Phonics	50	____	____
Morphology – word structure and derivations	50	____	____
Word meanings	50	____	____
Sentence-level knowledge			
Word classes and cohesion	60	____	____
Sentence types and structure	60	____	____
Punctuation	30	____	____
Text-level knowledge			
Cohesion, layout and organisation	30	____	____
Fiction, non-fiction and poetry	70	____	____
Critical evaluation			
Ability to evaluate the quality of texts	25	____	____
How information and ideas are presented	25	____	____
Terminology (add up terminology scores from separate sections)	60	____	____

You may also want to compare your scores more broadly, across the main areas of English covered. This also enables you to compare your test with your audit. Use the following grid to do this. As you complete it, add up all your raw scores and divide by five to find out your *overall percentage* mark for the test. (Note: terminology is not included here as it falls within each separate section.)

Area of English	Maximum possible	Your raw score	Your percentage score
The nature and role of Standard English	30	____	____
The spoken and written language systems of English	20	____	____
Word-level knowledge	150	____	____
Sentence-level knowledge	150	____	____
Text-level knowledge	100	____	____
Critical evaluation of texts	50	____	____
ALL SECTIONS	500	____	____

Relate your separate and overall percentage test scores to the scale below. Remember, however, that all scores are relative to the nature of the material tested and the time at which the test took place. **This should therefore only be used as a rough guide, and not viewed as any kind of absolute standard.**

80-100%   In the areas tested, your score is very good and indicates that you probably meet the level expected of an English specialist. Well done!

60-80%   In the areas tested, your score is good and indicates that you probably meet the level expected of a non-English specialist. Some attention is necessary in places, but you probably have little to worry about.

50-60%   In the areas tested, your score is adequate and probably indicates that you are moving towards the level expected of a non-English specialist. However, further work is necessary on many or most aspects. You probably knew that already!

0-50%   In the areas tested, your score is rather low. Use the test positively to target the areas you need to work on – and really work on them. Remember, you only have to get there by the end of your training – nothing to worry about right now.

Consider also, however, as you move on to Part 6 – Setting Targets – how you *felt* as you tackled the test sections. Did you *know* the answers, or did you succeed by using logic? Clearly, if you think your score was higher (or lower) than it should have been for any reason, you need to take this into account. After all, it's the quality of your own knowledge and understanding that matters, not the scores themselves.

Part 5: Answers to test questions

The nature and role of standard English

1. (a) F (b) T (c) T (d) T (e) T (f) F (g) F (h) T (i) T (j) F
2. (a), (d), (e)
3. (b), (c)
4. (a) SE (b) NSE (c) SE (d) SE (e) NSE (f) SE
5. (a) dialect (b) accent
6. (a) dialect (chimley) (b) dialect (never/nowt) (c) dialect (brung), accent (yer)

   (d) accent (oi/'aven't/'im) (e) dialect (afeared) (f) dialect (went), accent (oot)

   (g) dialect (blethering)

The spoken and written language systems of English

1. (a) T (b) F (c) T (d) T (e) F (f) F
2. (a) spoken (b) written (c) spoken (d) spoken (e) spoken (f) written
3. **(a) written (b) spoken (c) written (d) written (e) written (f) spoken**

   (g) spoken (h) written

Knowledge at word level

Phonics and how the writing system represents the sound system

1. (a) F (b) T *(they can also refer to written letters)* (c) T (d) T (e) F *(there are about 44)*
2. Count any two of: you, through, crew, queue, view
3. emu 2; hippopotamus 5
4. onset **s**, rime **eal**; onset **d**, rime **uck**; no onset, rime **owl**
5. lion 4; bear 2 or 3 (depending on whether, in your accent, you pronounce the r or not); jackal 5; elephant 7; ape 2
6. **z**oo glasse**s** f**ie**ld ke**y** ra**g**e **j**ust
7. *Count any two of the following marked adjacent consonant groups:*

   When her **fr**ie**nd** le**ft**, **Fl**ora fe**lt** so sad that she began to **cr**y.
8. *Count any two of:* ele**ph**ant gori**ll**a ora**ng**-utan
9. *Count any two of:* **ow**l chimpanz**ee** **a**p**e** (a split digraph)
10. *Consonant trigraph:* ca**tch** or e**dge**

    Vowel trigraph: s**igh**
11. (a) height (b) caught or kit (c) toe

    (d) howl or frown (e) grown or frown (f) site or mate
12. *Count any two of:* h**ow**l s**ay** b**oy**
13. gramm**a**r sent**e**nce mis**e**ry *(unstressed vowels often give rise to spelling confusion)*
14. /ə /

15 *In order:* phoneme; grapheme; digraph; trigraph; syllable; onset; rime; segment; blend; reversible

Morphology – word structure and derivations

1 (a) T   (b) T   (c) F   (d) F   (e) T

2 arrowhead, headlight, redhead, headteacher

3 *Latin:* submarine, innate, century, circumnavigate

   Greek: psychology, phoneme, alphabet, grammar

4 sauna – Finnish; mutton – French; apartheid – Afrikaans; potato – Spanish; whisky – Gaelic; algebra – Arabic; kindergarten – German; shampoo – Hindi;

5 (a) prefix: un   root: wrap(p)   suffix: ing

   (b) prefix: pre   root: cede   (no suffix)

   (c) (no prefix)   root: strange   suffix: ness

   (d) prefix: sub   root: tract   suffix: ion

6 (a) extra/outside   (b) dis/not   (c) intra/within   (d) inter/between

7 result**s** – plural noun; Jason**'s** – possessive form of singular noun; high**est** – superlative adjective; scor**ed** – past tense verb; high**er** – comparative adjective

8 (a) rigidity (b) goodness (c) brighten (d) energetic (e) rapidly

   Note: suffixes are often a clue to word class

9 *In order:* morphology, morpheme, root, compound word, prefix, suffix, inflection

Word meanings and how words relate to each other

1 (a) T   (b) F   (c) T   (d) F   (e) T

2 (a) row/row   (b) brake/break   (c) rush/hurry   (d) tiny/enormous

3 cross, plant, play, shoot, foot, cricket

4 A: pretty/handsome/beautiful

   B: lively/energetic/active

   C: intelligent/bright/quick-witted/clever

5 *In order:* (a) freezing, cold, tepid, warm, hot   (b) whisper, mutter, say, call, shout

6 pram/perambulator; zoo/zoological gardens; vet/veterinary surgeon

7 I'm hard up; I'm skint; I need some kip; Shut up!; Let's chill out; I'm broke

8 *Count any three of:* I'm hard up; I'm skint; I have no money; I'm broke

9 *Broadly, you want to replace the colloquialisms which you have identified with words or phrases such as those below. You may have found other acceptable alternatives.*

   Gemma: **Hello/good morning**, Gemma here!

   Sara: It's Sara. Just thought I'd **call you/give you a call/telephone you** to **find out about/learn more about** Pete and Gill.

   Gemma: **Wait a moment** – I'll just switch the **television** off.

10 (You must) stop crying now. *(or similar)*

11 Synonym (d), colloquialism (g), acronym (c), homonym (e), homograph (a), antonym (b), homophone (f)

   Note: homonyms are often interpreted more loosely, to incorporate homophones and homographs.

Sentence level knowledge – grammar and punctuation

Word classes and cohesion within a sentence

1   (a) F   (b) T   (c) F   (d) T   (e) T

2   *Note that sometimes a word is included in more than one word class.*

(a)	proper noun	Charles/Jo/Peter Robbins
(b)	abstract noun	surprise/delight
(c)	concrete noun	play/meal/restaurant/diners/members/cast/man/table
(d)	collective noun	cast
(e)	verb	was/went/found/included/was sitting
(f)	adverb	extremely
(g)	pronoun	their/they/theirs
(h)	preposition	following/for/to/of/at
(i)	conjunction	and/where
(j)	determiner	the/a/their/other/next
(k)	adjective	enjoyable/well-known/local/other/leading/next
(l)	relative pronoun	which

3   3rd person

4   (a) pronouns

5   past tense

6   (b) nouns and verbs

7   (a) **am going**   main verb form: going   auxiliary: am

     (b) **will have finished**.   main verb form: finished   auxiliary: will have

     (c) **May + go**   main verb form: go   auxiliary: may

8   (a) non-finite   (b) finite   (c) finite

     Finite verbs indicate a distinction in tense or person.

9   *Noun phrase – choose one of:* the white horse, my mum, the boy carrying the suitcase

     Prepositional phrase: after the famous hurricane

     Note: 'the famous hurricane', 'the boy' and 'the suitcase' are also noun phrases in their own right, embedded within longer phrases.

10   (a) verb   (b) noun   (c) noun   (d) adjective   (e) adverb   (f) preposition

11   *The verbs you need to replace are the bland* **said** *and* **went**. *Many alternatives are possible, such as (for 'said')* shouted/grumbled/yelled/screamed/insisted/grunted; *and (for 'went')* ran/rushed/stamped/stomped/stalked *etc. Decide whether you deserve your two marks or not!*

12   *Again, make your own decision. The noun phrase is* **a dog.** *Expand to something like:*

     I have **a hairy, yappy little dog** which is very friendly.

     I have **a black dog with floppy ears**, which is very friendly.

13   **Those men are** eating **our pizzas**. *Must be all correct.*

14   (a) (i)   (b) (iv)   (c) (iii)   (d) (ii)

     (e) (iv)   (f) (iii)   (g) (ii)   (h) (i)

15   (a) noun   (b) determiner   (c) nouns   (d) verbs   (e) verbs   (f) conjunctions   (g) adjective

     (h) pronoun   (i) adverb   (j) preposition

Sentence types and structure

1 (a) F   (b) T   (c) T   (d) F   (e) F

2 (a) question (b) statement (c) command (d) command (e) exclamation

3 *Alternatives are possible. You might have something like:*

(a) *Command*: Eat the last biscuit. *OR* Eat the last biscuit! (*tells someone what to do*)

(b) *Statement*: You have eaten the last biscuit. (*statement of fact*)

4 (a) phrase   (b) phrase   (c) clause   (d) phrase

Clause needs a subject–verb relationship.

5 *Subject:* The older children   *Predicate:* were studying algebra

6 *Subject:* The older children   *Verb:* were studying   *Object:* algebra

7 *Subject:* Ms Peters   *Verb:* dismissed   *Object:* the class

Adverbial: as quickly as possible

8 *Your sentence will be the same, but with a replacement for Ms Peters. For example:*

As quickly as possible, **the exasperated caretaker** dismissed the class.

9 *Your sentence will be the same, but in a slightly different order:*

Ms Peters dismissed the class **as quickly as possible**.

Ms Peters, **as quickly as possible**, dismissed the class. (*note need for commas*)

10 *Again, various options are possible, for example:*

Mr Sharp **lay** down, **emptied** his briefcase and **tossed** a file to the Inspector.

However, you don't get marks for simply filling the blanks here.

Transitive verbs – (b) and (c); intransitive verb (a) (*whatever words you've put!*)

Transitive verbs take an object.

11 (a)   (c)   (d)

12 *The main clause is underlined below; the subordinate clause is italicised.*

a) **Freddie**, *who had rather enjoyed the free wine,* **felt frivolous**.

b) *After I finish writing up my assignment,* **I'm going to watch a horror film.**

c) **Cordelia has not done her homework** *because she left her notebook in school.*

13 (a) complex   (b) complex   (c) simple   (d) compound

Simple sentence has one main clause; compound sentence has two or more main clauses; complex sentence has main and subordinate clause(s).

Embedded clause is in sentence (a).

14 and – C; when – S; although – S; if – S; or – C

15 if, while, because

16 whose, who, which

17 (a) subject   (b) predicate   (c) object

(d) simple sentence   (e) compound sentence   (f) complex sentence

Punctuation

1 (a) F   (b) T   (c) T   (d) T   (e) F

2 *Remember: 2 marks if sentence is completely correct, 1 mark if one mistake only. Take care to check every single mark.*

(a) He brought me a bar of chocolate, some crisps and a bottle of white wine.

Sometimes a colon heads a list, and sometimes semi-colons are used to separate longer items in a list. However this is less appropriate in a short list of this sort.

(b) 'Go and apologise,' said Mrs Taylor, 'and offer to help tidy up.'

(c) Christopher, who had finished his lunch by ten o'clock, had nothing left to eat.

(d) *Alternatives possible:* 'Mum, help!' cried Sally. 'Mum – help!' cried Sally. 'Mum! Help!' cried Sally.

(e) Although the war ended in 1945**,** its repercussions were felt for a very long time afterwards**.**

3 (a) After lunch, we went to the park, **which** was deserted.

After lunch, we went to the park**. It** was deserted.

After lunch, we went to the park**; it** was deserted. *(Replace comma in run-on sentence with grammatically more appropriate punctuation.)*

(b) 'Mum**,** can we go out to play now?' asked Rosie. *(Add comma.)*

(c) We had **sausages** and roast potatoes. *(Apostrophes not needed for plural.)*

(d) No! That can't be true! *(Extra full stop omitted.)*

(e) Becky's cat was licking **its** kittens. *(Apostrophe not needed in possessive pronoun.)*

4 (c)

5 *The following alterations change the meaning substantially:*

(a) After he had eaten my dog, Sam was violently sick on the carpet.

(b) If you're unsure, don't ask me what to do.

(c) The teacher punished the boys for no good reason. They told their parents.

(d) Trolls usually smell. Nasty children are afraid of them.

6 apostrophe (d)   semi-colon (e)   full stop (c)   exclamation mark (b)   comma (a)

Textual knowledge

Cohesion, layout and organisation

1 (a) T   (b) T   (c) F   (d) T   (e) F

2 (c)   (a)   (d)   (b)   (e)

3 *Connectives:* however, also, in contrast

Pronouns: its, it, this, these *(any three)*

4 Tom opened the heavy, iron gate and **he (alternatively, could be omitted)** saw something incredible – a tropical beach! The sun was golden, like a red-hot fireball, and the sea **was** gleaming like a million sapphire jewels. It was out of this world! Tom decided to walk along the sandy shore. Suddenly **he** saw a little golden key in the sand, and picked it up.

5 *You'd recognise them all at a glance, wouldn't you? So if all are ticked – one point.*

6 (a)   (c)   (d)   (f)

7 (i) *Paragraph 2 would start after* **meantime**. *Paragraph 3 would start after* **again**.

(ii) *Paragraph 2 would start after* **teaching**. *Paragraph 3 would start after* **strand**.

8 (a) text (i)   (d) text (ii)

Fiction, non-fiction and poetry

1 (a) F   (b) F   (c) F   (d) T   (e) T

2 (a) P   (b) NF   (c) NF   (d) F

3 (a) orientation   (b) problem   (c) development (also called complication)   (d) climax

(e) resolution   (f) ending

4   (a) fable   (b) historical fiction   (c) myth   (d) adventure story   (e) legend   (f) fairy tale

5   (i) fairy tale   (ii) historical fiction   (iii) fable

6   (a) (ii)   (b) (i)   (c) (ii)   (d) (i) or (iii)   (e) (i) or (iii)   (f) (iii)

7   (a) discussion   (b) recount   (c) non-chronological report

8   If you've picked out the starting and finishing statement you can have the marks!

Start (e)   End (c)   *Statement (d) would probably come second. The various arguments could be ordered in various ways.*

9   (i) explanation   (ii) instructions   (iii) recount

10   (a) (i) is best   (b) (i), (ii) or (iii)   (c) (i)   (d) (ii)   (e) (iii)

11   (a) narrative poem   (b) blank verse   (c) limerick   (d) calligram   (e) haiku

12   *Various options are possible. You might have answers such as:*

not written in conventional sentences; lots of imagery; lines are of varied length; not chronological

13   *simile:* like a lightning bolt, like a demon breathing out fire, like a madman

metaphor: a great green dragon, a metal monster

alliteration: **gr**eat **gr**een, **m**etal **m**onster, **sp**itting out **sp**arks, **scr**eeching and **scr**eaming, **l**ike a **l**ightning bolt

onomatopoeia: hissing, spitting, clanging, banging, crashing, flashing, screeching, screaming

internal rhyme: clanging and banging, crashing and flashing

assonance: l**i**ke a l**igh**tning bolt, h**i**ssing and sp**i**tting, d**e**mon br**ea**thing, scr**ee**ching and scr**ea**ming

14   *In order:* plot, theme, voice, viewpoint, style

15   (a) alliteration   (b) onomatopoeia   (c) metaphor   (d) personification

16   (a) discussion   (b) explanation   (c) recount   (d) instruction text
(e) non-chronological report   (f) persuasive text

Critical evaluation of texts

Evaluating the quality of texts

As already mentioned, subjectivity abounds in the area of textual evaluation. Literature cannot be judged simply on the basis of a list of criteria – there's far more to it than that. However, by starting to think about what criteria you might apply to different types of book, you're making a start.

1   (a) R   (b) R, P, H   (c) P   (d) H   (e) R, P, H   (f) P, H   (g) P, H   (h) P, H   (i) R   (j) P   (k) P
(l) R   (m) P, H   (n) P, H   (o) H

2   *Likewise, you may have many criticisms of these texts which are not listed here – give yourself a mark if you feel confident you can justify your comments, to a maximum of 10. Here are 15 negative comments:*

(a) content banal and boring
      title does not reflect content
(b) first sentences don't instruct at all – inappropriate
      sequence not accurate

very imprecise

tone too personal

(c) content uninteresting

every line finishes with a full stop

language structures stilted and unnatural (especially the speech)

does not use speech punctuation

(d) descriptive language 'over the top' – could you read a whole novel like this?

sentences long and complicated to follow

imprecise use of pronoun – who is 'he'?

(e) out of date

inaccurate

An awareness of how information and ideas are presented and can be interpreted in different ways, depending on point of view, context, purpose and audience

1   (a) (iv)   (b) (i)   (c) (ii)   (d) (iii)   (e) (ii)   (f) (iii)   (g) (i)   (h) (iv)

2   Four of (a)   (b)   (d)   (g)   (h)

3   (a) fact   (b) fact   (c) opinion   (d) opinion

4   (ii), (iv), (v)

5   (a) (ii)   (b) (v)   (c) (iv) [also to some degree (ii)]   (d) (iv)

6   *An opportunity for creative writing to finish off … As long as you're sure you've written a clearly one-sided headline, give yourself the marks. You might have something on these lines:*

(a) Southampton shame Anfield stars

(b) Saints steal a result – Liverpool unlucky

Part 6: Targets for further development

Target-setting has become part of the way that schools work – each school sets targets for its own performance, while teachers are constantly involved in setting targets for children, as a way of helping pupils know what they need to master next. So as a teacher you'll soon be involved in target-setting for and with others on a regular basis. While studying for your teaching qualification, you may also be set targets, or asked to identify targets for yourself.

On the basis of your performance in **both the audit and test:** formally record your targets for professional development below; make **clear** and **specific** reference to any areas which clearly require attention; ensure you indicate **where, when and how the targets will be achieved**; remember to monitor your progress and check that you have succeeded in addressing your development areas.

Area of English	Your targets (refer explicitly to areas within your audit and test results)	Your study plan – resources, dates
The nature and role of standard English		
The spoken and written language systems of English		
Word-level knowledge		
Sentence-level knowledge		
Text-level knowledge		
Critical evaluation of texts		

Targets for further development

What evidence will indicate that you have achieved your targets?

Part 7: Revision and further reading

Suggestions for revision

Through the audit and test, you should now be able to identify those areas in which you're performing at a satisfactory level and those in which further study is needed. How should you go about this?

Breaking down the task into small, manageable sections that you can tackle bit by bit is the key. If you prioritise the areas in need of improvement, you can then plan to devote most time and effort to the areas of English in which you are weakest. Draw up a study plan as outlined in Part 6, clearly specifying the areas on which you need to focus, and when you will do this. Also decide *how* you are going to do your revision. What books will you need? Will you have to buy these or can you borrow them? Might you be able to use any Internet resources? Have you any friends or family with whom you can discuss these areas of English?

When you have drawn up your study plan, make sure you stick to it. Although you have until the end of your ITT course to meet the standards, you will have a huge number of other commitments, so you need to be firm about keeping your subject knowledge revision on schedule. If you can, start your revision before you commence your course. This will stand you in very good stead – you can then focus less on the subject knowledge itself, and more on learning how to teach it, during your course.

You may find it useful to monitor your progress by referring back on a regular basis to your original audit and test. How do you feel *now* about your knowledge, interest and confidence? How much more secure do you feel about your ability to answer the questions? Re-test yourself to compare your scores (and your feelings of confidence) – do you now meet the grade in all areas?

Further reading

Crystal, D. (2003) *The Cambridge Encyclopedia of the English Language* (2nd ed.). Cambridge: Cambridge University Press.

Eyres, I. (2000) *Developing Subject Knowledge: Primary English.* London: Paul Chapman Publishing.

MacArthur, T. (ed.) (2005) *Concise Oxford Companion to the English Language*. Oxford: Oxford University Press.

Medwell, J., Moore, G., Wray, D. and Griffiths, V. (2007) *Primary English: Knowledge and Understanding* (3rd ed.). Exeter: Learning Matters.

Medwell, J. and Wray, D. (2007) *Primary English: Extending Knowledge in Practice*. Exeter: Learning Matters.

Medwell, J., Wray, D., Minns, H., Griffiths, V. and Coates, L. (2007) *Primary English: Teaching Theory and Practice* (3rd ed.). Exeter: Learning Matters.

Randall, E. and Hardman, A. (2002) *A–Z of Key Concepts in Primary English*. Exeter: Learning Matters.

Wilson, A. (2004) *Language Knowledge for Primary Teachers* (3rd ed.). London: David Fulton Publishers.

Online reference sources

Some useful online sources of information are now available, particularly in the area of grammar.

DfES (2000) *Grammar for Teachers*. Available at
http://www.standards.dfes.gov.uk/primary/profdev/

Hughes, A. (1995) *On-line English Grammar.* Available at
http://www.edufind.com/english/grammar/index. cfm

Myhill, D. (2006) *Cybergrammar*. University of Exeter. Available at
http://www.cybergrammar.co.uk/

University College, London (1998) *The Internet Grammar of English.* Available at
http://www.ucl.ac.uk/internet-grammar/home.htm

ACHIEVING QTS

The Achieving QTS series continues to grow, with nearly 50 titles across a range of strands. Our titles address issues of teaching and learning across both primary and secondary phases in a highly practical and accessible manner, making each title an invaluable resource for trainee teachers.

We've updated and improved 13 of our bestselling titles in line with the new Standards for QTS (September 2007). These titles are highlighted with a * in the list below.

Assessment for Learning and Teaching in Primary Schools
Mary Briggs, Angela Woodfield, Cynthia Martin and Peter Swatton
£15   176 pages   ISBN: 978 1 90330 074 9

Assessment for Learning and Teaching in Secondary Schools
Martin Fautley and Jonathan Savage
£16   160 pages   ISBN: 978 1 84445 107 4

*Learning and Teaching in Secondary Schools (third edition)
Viv Ellis
£16   192 pages   ISBN: 978 1 84445 096 1

Learning and Teaching Using ICT in Secondary Schools
John Woollard
£17.50   176 pages   ISBN: 978 1 84445 078 7

Passing the ICT Skills Test (second edition)
Clive Ferrigan
£8   80 pages   ISBN: 978 1 84445 028 2

Passing the Literacy Skills Test
Jim Johnson
£8   80 pages   ISBN: 978 1 90330 012 1

Passing the Numeracy Skills Test (third edition)
Mark Patmore,
£8   64 pages   ISBN: 978 1 90330 094 7

*Primary English: Audit and Test (third edition)
Doreen Challen
£9   64 pages   ISBN: 978 1 84445 110 4

*Primary English: Knowledge and Understanding (third edition)
Jane Medwell, George Moore, David Wray and Vivienne Griffiths
£16   240 pages   ISBN: 978 1 84445 093 0

*Primary English: Teaching Theory and Practice (third edition)
Jane Medwell, David Wray, Hilary Minns, Vivienne Griffiths and Liz Coates
£16   208 pages   ISBN: 978 1 84445 092 3

*Primary ICT: Knowledge, Understanding and Practice (third edition)
Jonathan Allen, John Potter, Jane Sharp and Keith Turvey
£16   256 pages   ISBN: 978 1 84445 094 7

*Primary Mathematics: Audit and Test (third edition)
Claire Mooney and Mike Fletcher
£9   52 pages   ISBN: 978 1 84445 111 1

*Primary Mathematics: Knowledge and Understanding (third edition)
Claire Mooney, Lindsey Ferrie, Sue Fox, Alice Hansen and Reg Wrathmell
£16   176 pages   ISBN: 978 1 84445 053 4

*Primary Mathematics: Teaching Theory and Practice (third edition)
Claire Mooney, Mary Briggs, Mike Fletcher, Alice Hansen and Judith McCullouch
£16   192 pages   ISBN: 978 1 84445 099 2

*Primary Science: Audit and Test (third edition)
John Sharp and Jenny Byrne
£9   80 pages   ISBN: 978 1 84445 109 8

*Primary Science: Knowledge and Understanding (third edition)
Graham Peacock, John Sharp, Rob Johnsey and Debbie Wright
£16   240 pages   ISBN: 978 1 84445 098 5

*Primary Science: Teaching Theory and Practice (third edition)
John Sharp, Graham Peacock, Rob Johnsey, Shirley Simon and Robin Smith
£16   144 pages   ISBN: 978 1 84445 097 8

*Professional Studies: Primary and Early Years (third edition)
Kate Jacques and Rob Hyland
£16   256 pages   ISBN: 978 1 84445 095 4

Teaching Arts in Primary Schools
Raywen Ford, Stephanie Penny, Lawry Price and Susan Young
£15   192 pages   ISBN: 978 1 90330 035 0

Teaching Design and Technology at Key Stages 1 and 2
Gill Hope
£17   224 pages   ISBN: 978 1 84445 056 5

Teaching Foundation Stage
Iris Keating
£15   200 pages   ISBN: 9 781 90330 033 6

Teaching Humanities in Primary Schools
Editor: Pat Hoodless
£15   192 pages   ISBN: 978 1 90330 036 7

Achieving QTS Cross-Curricular Strand

Children's Spiritual, Moral, Social and Cultural Development
Tony Eaude
£14   128 pages   ISBN: 978 1 84445 048 0

Creativity in Primary Education
Anthony Wilson
£15   224 pages   ISBN: 978 1 84445 013 8

Creativity in Secondary Education
Jonathan Savage, Martin Fautley
£16   144 pages   ISBN: 978 1 84445 0732

Teaching Citizenship in Primary Schools
Editor: Hilary Claire
£15   192 pages   ISBN: 978 1 84445 010 7

Teaching Literacy Across the Primary Curriculum
David Wray
£14   144 pages   ISBN: 978 1 84445 008 4

Achieving QTS Extending Knowledge in Practice

Extending Knowledge in Practice: Primary English
Jane Medwell and David Wray
£16   160 pages   ISBN: 978 1 84445 104 3

Extending Knowledge in Practice: Primary ICT
John Duffty
£16   176 pages   ISBN: 978 1 84445 055 8

Extending Knowledge in Practice: Primary Mathematics:
Alice Hansen
£16   176 pages   ISBN: 978 1 84445 054 1

Extending Knowledge in Practice: Primary Science
Judith Roden, Hellen Ward and Hugh Ritchie
£16   160 pages   ISBN: 978 1 84445 106 7

Achieving QTS Practical Handbooks

Learning and Teaching with Interactive Whiteboards: Primary and Early Years
David Barber, Linda Cooper, Graham Meeson
£14   128 pages   ISBN: 978 1 84445 081 7

Learning and Teaching with Virtual Learning Environments
Helena Gillespie, Helen Boulton, Alison Hramiak and Richard Williamson
£14   144 pages   ISBN: 978 1 84445 076 3

*Successful Teaching Placement: Primary and Early Years (second edition)
Jane Medwell
£12   160 pages   ISBN: 978 1 84445 091 6

Using Resources to Support Mathematical Thinking: Primary and Early Years
Doreen Drews and Alice Hansen
£15   160 pages   ISBN: 978 1 84445 057 2

Achieving QTS Reflective Readers

Primary English Reflective Reader
Andrew Lambirth
£14   128 pages   ISBN: 978 1 84445 035 0

Primary Mathematics Reflective Reader
Louise O'Sullivan, Andrew Harris, Gina Donaldson, Gill Bottle, Margaret Sangster and Jon Wild
£14   120 pages   ISBN: 978 1 84445 036 7

Primary Professional Studies Reflective Reader
Sue Kendall-Seater
£15   192 pages   ISBN: 978 1 84445 033 6

Primary Science Reflective Reader
Judith Roden
£14   128 pages   ISBN: 978 1 84445 037 4

Primary Special Educational Needs Reflective Reader
Sue Soan
£14   136 pages   ISBN: 978 1 84445 038 1

Secondary Professional Studies Reflective Reader
Simon Hoult
£14   192 pages   ISBN: 978 1 84445 034 3

Secondary Science Reflective Reader
Gren Ireson and John Twidle
£16   128 pages   ISBN: 978 1 84445 065 7

To order please phone our order line 0845 230 9000 or send an official order or cheque to
BEBC, Albion Close, Parkstone, Poole, BH12 3LL
Order online at www.learningmatters.co.uk